Written by Alexandra Elle

Illustrated by Ashleigh Kinsey

© 2013 by Alexandra Elle

Words from a Wanderer: Notes & Love Poems
By: Alexandra Elle
To my little Bunni.

"All that is gold does not glitter,
Not all those who wander are lost;
The old that is strong does not wither,
Deep roots are not reached by the frost.

From the ashes a fire shall be woken,
A light from the shadows shall spring;
Renewed shall be blade that was broken,
The crownless again shall be king.

- J.R.R. Tolkien, The Fellowship of the Ring

At twenty-three I am now aware that I'm not crazy nor am I the only person in the world who talks to themselves. Writing has been a passion of mine since before I can remember. Being able to put words on paper has been a saving grace because many days I cannot find the words to say out loud—so I write them down. This little book is a compilation of some comforting things I've had to tell myself to get through the toughest days of my life. I remember there was a period of time that I didn't write, I couldn't and it was mainly because I didn't want to. It was nerve wracking to face my truth and I was extremely hard on myself for making so many mistakes. I learned a lot during the silence. My pages were blank but my mind was on fire. When I picked up a pen and started to write again, my work was different. It wasn't filled with sorrow, anxiety, hurt or fear. My words started to become comforting, full of understanding, honesty and forgiveness. I started writing notes to myself because a little self-love can go a long way. I no longer seek validation from others nor do I rely on the outside world to tell me how worthy I am or how amazing I can be. I have finally fallen in love with myself and it's the best feeling on earth to wake up and know that I am truly loved from the inside out.

-Alex Elle

#anote2self

Dear Self,
I know you struggle sometimes but just in case I don't tell you enough, you're beautiful. Thank you for being so strong and transparent. The world sees you even when you feel invisible. I appreciate your heart and your stubbornness. Your willingness to love even after being discarded and forgotten is admirable. I am so proud to know that you've grown to acknowledge your worth.
With Love,
Self

Resilient Self,
Your past was practice. The mistakes you've made along the way have motivated your mission! Trust and believe that you're on the right track.
Love Always,
Self

• • • • • • • • • • • • • • • • • •

Courageous Self,
Make an effort to finish what you start. You know from experience that giving up has gotten you nowhere. Work harder than you think you did yesterday!
Much Love,
Self

• • • • • • • • • • • • • • • • • •

The heart is resilient and forgiving. It is the mind that causes us stress.

Dear Self,
Seasons change. People grow together and apart. Life moves
on. You will be OK. Embrace it.
Hugs,
Self

. . . .

Dear Self,
You are not that broken or that battered. You're not that
bruised and your spirit isn't shattered. Keep in mind how
resilient you really are. Do not allow fear from your past
experiences disable your courage in the future.
Don't be afraid,
Self

. . . .

Worthy Self,
You are not just a "play thing" or an option on anyone's
roster. You are not disposable or unimportant. You are
worthy of time, gentleness and adoration. Please do not settle
or worry. Timing is everything and there is a love waiting
especially for you.
Be patient,
Self

Dream Chaser

I get angry with him when I wake and he's no longer there.
I curse the fact that he visits at night then flees in the
morning before the rising of a new sun.

My heart aches for the last kiss that I never get. He always
vanishes before I'm given the chance to loosen my grip from
his fingertips.

He stays patient when I fly off the handle. He knows I want
him to stay so I am ensured by his words that my heart he has
no intent to trample.

Calmly he repeats, every morning when I call yelling, "I'm
right where you left me, you're the one who leaves."

I guess it's not his fault that he can't come with me when I
awake from my dreams.

Dear Self

Dear Self,
If you keep going backwards with the same people that
God has intentionally removed from your life, you will
continue to stay stuck. There is no joy in being confused and
unhappy. Get rid of old bad habits and leave them where they
belong. What is meant for you will be yours. Learn to let go.
Dysfunction isn't love.
Sincerely,
Self

Dear Self,
Continue to walk in your purpose. Allow God to guide your
footsteps and positivity will lead your thoughts.
Love,
Self

Dear Self,
I am glad you are learning to be quiet. You're amazing with words but sometimes in the midst of not so beautiful times silence is golden.
Love,
Self

Shhh!

Reflect

As he awakens his mane flows freely; pieces of which are still intertwined in his Queen's fingers. He doesn't mind that her grip is tight when it comes to him.

He watches her sleep with love in his eyes; wondering why it took so long for him to see such a beautiful reflection.

Dear Self,
Know your boundaries and respect your limits. Sometimes the answer to others has to be "no." If you keep overextending yourself you will have nothing left to give when the time is right.
Love,
Self

Dear Self,
I do not thank you enough for evolving into such a strong person, mother, daughter and friend. I love you. Most days I overlook how far you've come. Keep sowing seeds of peace and continue to be the resilient woman that I know you are.
Always and forever,
Self

Dear Self,
They don't have to believe you now. You'll show them. Don't say a word.
Love,
Self

Raise your sons to respect women, your daughters to respect themselves and vice versa.

Raise your daughters to love their sisters so that one day they can work together without competition in mind.

Show your sons what love looks like. Allow them to cry and grow so they can blossom and become men who are not scared of emotions but compassionate toward the feelings of others.

Our children are sacred.

Try to set an amazing foundation for them the best way you know how.

Dear Self,
It's important that we start to respect one another because when we do love will follow.
Love,
Self

Dear Self,
Assumptions will ruin your beautiful mind. Be aware of what you're entertaining even in thought.
Love and Light,
Self

Dear Self,
Listen, learn, love and live. You owe yourself knowledge and peace.
Blessings,
Self

Hell and Back: Devil Dance, PT 1.

When you've lived in hell life becomes a bit easier to stomach
and a tad bit sweeter to swallow.

The little things don't wear you down as much and the
burdens of daily struggles seem to be accomplished with ease.

I've been to hell and back—it wasn't as hot there as I had
imagined.

Maybe that was because my soul was already set on fire or my
heart had been torched and scarred with burns by past lovers.

I wasn't sure why the temperature didn't bother me.

I walked around barefoot with the devil and wasn't sure how I
ended up hand in hand with him.

On any account, it wasn't on purpose...

He showed me around and we bartered my soul.

I didn't want to stay there but he wouldn't let me go.

Dear Self,

Please do not be foolish. People treat you how you allow them to. If you want different results stop settling with the same people and for the same things. If you want to see a change in your existence, be the change. Life isn't as complicated as we make it and love isn't as hard as we claim it is. If you want something, work for it. Be honest in your actions and give the world great reasons to love you. Smile at yourself every once in a while just because. Continue being great, generous and grand.

Love,

Self

Dear Self,

You have been doubted, hated, talked about, made fun of, hurt, lied to, lied on, broken and at your wits end. With that being said, I commend you for the fact that you are still standing. Your courage speaks volumes! I know your struggle and the pain you've endured. You are more than a conqueror. I am proud to say that your heart belongs to me. Nothing can keep you down and no one can steal your joy. All of your storms have ended up blessing the sky with rainbows. Don't give up, continue to stand tall and love yourself first.

You are appreciated,

Self

There is no love without respect.
There isn't much truth if spoken without genuine honesty. People are sometimes unaware that certain things go hand in hand. If you're going to talk about it, be about it. Try not to be selective in your actions. Be who you say you are. It's important that we learn, teach and allow our mind, body and spirit to work together with one another.

Dear Self,
Sometimes we have to learn to love when all odds are against us. Have a discerning heart, open mind and forgiving spirit. The beautiful thing about growth is the ability to see our changes. Embrace your seasons and watch them evolve in ways you couldn't imagine.
Peace,
Self

Dear Self,
When you live in love and light you will not go unseen. Ignite the world with every flame of your being.
Love,
Self

Dear Self,
Thank you for learning not to fear the lightning that may cause a disturbance in your life. Your failures, mistakes, lessons and turbulence have made your journey that much brighter and worthwhile.
Love always,
Self

Perfection isn't welcomed here; I'd like to see your flaws.
The blueprint of your beauty makes me want to love them all...

Dear Self,

You are a Queen, so even when they push you, don't take your crown off.

Love,

Self

Dear Self,

There is so much more to this life than just "this life."
Venture out and experience the beauty in living...

Beautifully yours,

Self

Dear Self,

Keep in mind that the reason you know you can be good to others is only because you've taken strides to be better for and to yourself.

Gratefully yours,

Self

<u>Some Timing</u>

Sometimes I don't think I am pretty but
some days I smile when I pass the mirror.
Sometimes I don't feel worthy but
then I look at my reflection and see my daughter, mother and
grandmother who are worthy of all things. That in itself says
a lot about me.
Some days I don't want anything to do with anyone but
then I remember who's been there for me when I've had no
one.
Sometimes life sucks. Other times not so much.
I've come to the conclusion that I need balance in my life so
these "sometimey" feelings are welcomed to stay.
If everything was all good all of the time I would be
miserable. And if everything was all bad I'd feel the same.
My ups and downs are reminiscent of yin and yang; they need
each other to help me get through the good and bad days.

Loving Self,
No matter how bad you want a person, if your hearts are in
two different places, you'll have to pass and move on.
Love,
Self

• • • • • • • • • • • • • • • • • •

Generous Self,
Yes, you are giving but do not give people the power to steal
your peace. It belongs to you and no one should be able to
run away with it.
Love,
Self

• • • • • • • • • • • • • • • • • •

Hesitant Self,
Love your neighbor even the ones who do not show you
the same courtesy. You can't expect to receive love if you're
selective and not really willing to give it. What you put into
the world you will indeed get back. Even if it's not from the
person you're expecting it to be.
Love,
Self

• • • • • • • • • • • • • • • • • •

I am a strong believer that enabling/putting up with mistreatment dictates how we may feel about ourselves. You have to ask yourself, "What am I missing and/or seeking?" You may love and want someone but who do you want and love more, them or yourself? Letting go is sometimes essential in growing up. Learn to truly love yourself first. Once that happens there will be no question about what's for you and what's not.

#anote2self

Dear Self,

There's a blessing in every breath you take. Even when it's hard to breathe you have yet to suffocate. I commend you for your endurance even when the air is thick—keep breathing, keep loving, keep going.

Love,
Self

Dear Self,

When you are truly stunning, gorgeous and beautiful, you won't have to prove that to anyone visually.

Love,
Self

Dear Self,

When you really love someone your heart might always beat for them. Just because that is true it doesn't mean that they will always dance for you. Keep in mind that you don't have to stop the rhythm just adjust the pace.

Love,
Self

Love yourself first. Buy your own flowers. Tell yourself how beautiful you are. Don't expect anyone to love you more than you do. When you meet a partner you shouldn't have expectations of flattery. The beautiful words and things will mean very little when you're already showering yourself with them first. Expectations can taint love when you're seeking to fill a void.

Dear Self,
Your king is coming. Please continue to be patient. You've kissed some frogs and you've learned some lessons. Now it's time to prepare yourself and Queendom for the ONE who is worthy. I know you get lonely and worried but fear not, your love is being prepared carefully and especially for you.

Love,
Self

Dear Self,

You will get what you genuinely bring to the table in a partnership. Bring love and communication to your table. Bring humility to your table along with honesty and trust. Use respect as your table cloth. That's the perfect table setting and if your partner can cook, well, there ya go! Often times we are what we attract and if you don't want messiness keep a clean house.

Love,
Self

Dear Self,

Find peace in silence.

Love,
Self

Dear Self,

I need you to learn how to forgive the ones who have wronged you. You say you do, you may even smile and wave but deep down you hoard hurt and distaste. It's important that you start to see the value of forgiveness. Not just for the sake of others but for your own. Being forgiving to those who you feel are "unworthy" does not make you weak. The ability to do so speaks to your heart and your character. Be wise and exude kindness despite if you feel as though someone is deserving or not. Your pride is bigger than you sometimes but that alone will continue to keep you guarded and unsatisfied. You cannot expect to be forgiven if you're not willing to have a yielding love toward your neighbor.

Love,
Self

One day you will have to be OK with the fact that they are never coming back.

There will come a time that you will stop counting the seconds, minutes, hours and days of their return.

You won't wait by the phone forever knowing that it's not going to ring and be the person you're longing for.

Eventually jumping when your phone buzzes with a text, that you want to be from them, will be a thing of the past—trust me, missing them will pass.

The bad memories may even fade to black eventually.

One day you will not hold a grudge for them bruising your heart and making you cry.

You will laugh at the little stupid lies they told you when trying to pull the wool over your eyes.

There will come a time when you don't look at the relationship as a regret but as a lesson.

You will stop holding them accountable for your misery and hurt and start smiling again.

The beauty in all the hurt is the resilience of the heart—trust me, you will love again.

There is no layaway in love.

You cannot beg and plead a person to give you what's rightfully theirs; especially if they aren't willing to share. If a man isn't ready to love you, let him be.

If a woman isn't prepared to give you her all, let her go.

Despite how much you think you want or need someone else, you don't.

Prepare yourself so that when the right one comes along you're ready and able to love them with your whole heart and not just pieces of it.

Comfort Zone

I seek refuge in you like I do my blanket on cold winter nights and even though you keep me warm. I still haven't a clue what love is like. We say it like we mean it but that's a learned behavior and both of us know we can't get too comfortable with being one another's savior.

• • • • • • • • • • • • • • • • •

Practice makes "perfect" but love makes it worth it.

• • • • • • • • • • • • • • • • •

Descend

He must've seen it falling...
Thank God for him. He didn't let it hit the ground. Instead he gently scooped it up and placed it back into my chest.
I guess I lost it in the midst of all the heartache...
I'm wondering if it fled because of the fear of breaking.
He wouldn't let it run away, unless it was with him.

Top 10

You don't have to apologize for how you feel.

Be true to who you are and honest to others.

If you are leading people on then it's time to let them go, be fair to the hearts you encounter.

Commit if you can and love if you want.

Do not make promises that you aren't willing to keep.

All intentions aren't good ones. Make sure you not only mean well but that you're doing well.

Think before you speak, it's OK to talk to yourself first.

If you're not really ready to commit don't force it.

Try not to run from your fears. Life teaches lessons, pay attention.

Let Me

Let me see you, come here.

Let me hold your hand and marvel at one of God's greatest creations.

I'm trying not to be biased because I love you but you're beautiful and I can't help but stare.

Take your time with me.

I am in no rush to pass the seconds that we spend because they turn into the minutes in which are ours to wallow in.

Can you see me?

My goose bumps will lead the way. Close your eyes and enjoy this selfish pride that only surrenders selfless to you.

Let me know you.

I will kneel humbly at your feet so that you know you can walk with me.

A king needs his queen, neither of which is superior.

Equally yoked — your rib, my backbone.

You exhale as I inhale the greatness you choose to share with me.

<u>Light</u>

A love so bright that it makes the sun and stars envy us.

<u>One in the same</u>

I know why they love him because I once loved him too.
To them he is their sunshine, with me, well; he just leaves me
an awkward shade of blue.
They gawk at his charisma and charming good looks
but to me he is a liar, a thief and a crook.
I know they think his love will never ever end
but when they cause him stress, he blindly flees to me again.
His colors are so radiant but his heart follows his wandering
eyes—
The trophies aren't enough for him if the prize doesn't shine.
His spirit is polyamorous and that is something he cannot
hide...
One won't suffice especially when he's done and had his fun.
They might be his moon today but tomorrow I'll be his sun.

Past Pleasures

You used to bury your head near my clavicle and inhale—I made sure I smelled as sweet as sugar just for you.

I often wonder if you long for my hands on the back of your neck or my fingertips dancing with your earlobe.

I miss you falling asleep in my lap. I could look at you all day.

That closeness made me care so much more.

Your faux love was my favorite drug and now these occasional withdrawals suck.

I think about you often but not enough to text and I wonder about your happiness but not enough to call and check.

Trying to force myself to remember has now become harder than encouraging my mind to forget.

Breathtaking

It doesn't matter that he loves me hard enough to hurt me.
The strength of his grasp refuses to loosen and the truth is, I
rather him not let me go.
He's the yes to my answers and the veins in which my blood
flows freely.
 Memorized by those coffee brown eyes; his skin color
reminds me of the sun's glow.
Sweet to the taste, he enables my lungs to inhale his naturally
fragrant scent of sexy.
His presence is a blessing that blesses me with more than just
love but pure heaven sent passion and admiration for a soul as
beautiful as his.
I'm dreaming of the day that I can have his last name and use
these hips to bear the seeds that he plants.
The slightest glance of him gives me chills and to know
that he adores me more than more is mind boggling, heart
stopping and wonderful.
It doesn't matter that he loves me hard enough to hurt me
because he won't.
The strength of his grasp tightens firmly around my torso
as we lay there pacing one another's breath with our bare
chests—he breathes and I follow, matching his heart rate to a T.
I believe in love now, it's breathtaking, unmistakably amazing
and soothing.
My dreams came true when I met you.

Enthralled

His intelligence is what wooed her in.
How he took interest in her art and not just her words.
How he memorized her story and could tell it with his mouth
closed. Hand in hers without a sound escaping his vocal
cords; it was that kind of connection.
He's earned her memory so now she considers his feelings,
remembers his actions and appreciates his effort.
She can tell he's got that good brain and she loves his
beautiful mind.

Treasure Torture

This isn't infatuation for me.
I am not sure what it is for him but I will not judge his heart-
-either way, either or.
These feelings aren't fleeting; they are steady and even.
Something that I have never experienced when engulfed in
the lust of others.
He encourages my thought process; he turns me up and on.

I am pleased to say that he just might even enhance my ability
to see love clearly.
Miles apart but I don't think light-years could keep me away.
He does laps within my memory and I'd prefer if he'd stay.
My heart wants him now or never but that's because she's new
to this.
I'll treasure him although it tortures her to fathom someone
else getting her first kiss.

Love isn't supposed to hurt us; it's meant to heal. You are worthy of the real thing. Find that mutual respect and adoration
will follow suit.

Sometimes it's not the physical person that I miss but
the energy we shared...

Dear Future Lover,
I'd like to meet you one day.
I often wonder what it would feel like to lay with you, to inhale your comfort and intertwine in the happiness of our silence. Maybe I'll get to kiss you and count the lines in your palm or miss you until I can't take anymore of you being gone. I hope you think about me and wonder where I am. I'd love to meet you one day but until then here I stand.

Potentially Yours,
Self

Dear Self,

If you ask and get no answer sometimes the silence that bounces back is the loudest truth. Be appreciative and open hearted to any stillness you receive. Everything isn't meant to be yours and everyone isn't worthy enough to hold a place in your space.

Quiet is Good,
Self

Dear Self,

Like the flowers in spring, I love how you always come back to life.
No matter the struggle you make it through. What a journey. What a blessing.

Grown Beautifully,
Self

I've been hurt so bad and I still love so hard. I admire my heart for that.

Believe in something greater than yourself.

Love a little harder.

Learn something different.

Let your feelings be.

Embrace the changes.

Cry when you want to.

Sob when you have to.

Share a smile with a stranger.

Laugh until your tummy hurts and cheeks ache.

Enjoy the moments of life even if they hurt.

Allow your heart to mend.

Be open to trusting again.

Your happiness is in your hands.

The Lost Art

C shaped, fingers linked, hearts humming from the rhythm of each beat.

Hair tousled, legs linked, lips lingering on the back of my neck.

Comforter half on, our bodies half hot.

The lost art of cuddling has me longing to paint a mural of this moment.

Staying broken never works because you will continue to
cut yourself.
I know what it feels like to be shattered but I am also familiar
with the amazing sensation of being pieced back together.
Do not beat yourself up; you are indeed allowed to fail
before succeeding.

•　•　•　•　•　•　•　•　•　•　•　•　•　•　•　•　•　•　•

I am not a fan of insects
but the butterflies he leaves behind
are more than welcomed to stay inside
and nestle in the pits of my belly.

•　•　•　•　•　•　•　•　•　•　•　•　•　•　•　•　•　•　•

Love without peace will leave you with nothing but chaos.
A peaceful love cannot exist without balance and respect.
Expect nothing and your spirit will accept all of the goodness
that's meant for you in this life.

•　•　•　•　•　•　•　•　•　•　•　•　•　•　•　•　•　•　•

When you meet your match in someone, even if it's not meant
to be a romantic connection, keep them close. Everyone is not
destined to be a part of your everyday but the ones who are
should be cherished and aware of their place in your life.

•　•　•　•　•　•　•　•　•　•　•　•　•　•　•　•　•　•　•

Be yourself wholeheartedly.

Speak the truth always.

Keep your word and back what you say with actions.

• • • • • • • • • • • • • • • • •

Give love a chance and don't expect perfection because you won't get it. Understand that there will be mistakes. Know what to hold onto and what to let go.

• • • • • • • • • • • • • • • • •

Don't bring tons of baggage to new spaces and experiences. Develop meaningful relationships with people you know are willing to match your effort. Everyone is not out to hurt you. Don't miss out on a beautiful thing because you're insecure. He isn't him and she isn't her. Allow people to prove to you that they are in it for the long run.

46

Vow

I sit and watch him closely.

I have a feeling that he thinks I am weird but that's OK.

His movements I have memorized and his smile warms my soul from the soles of my Chuck Taylors.

The warm sensation races up, up and away—past the heart that I love him with.

He's amazing.

I wish I could part my lips to speak but most moments I cannot.

He kisses me when he knows that love has got my tongue.

His beauty leaves me muted and all I can do is stare at the one man who deserves more than my left hand.

Pouring Peace

I had to learn to embrace the rain.

I needed to realize that cloudy days were sometimes more than alright.

Crying in the shower is where I felt most sane, most safe. The scorching hot water left welts on my brown skin but at least the dirty tears were given a place to be washed away.

I was ashamed and hurting for so long.

Hiding was my only option when the sunshine had taken heed to the horizon.

I am OK now.

The sunlight isn't the only thing that makes me happy anymore now that I can endure my storms.

The next few pages are for you to write. Encourage yourself to be amazing, let out your fears and be open to what comes to mind. If you'd like to share your notes join the conversation on Instagram by using the #ANote2Self hash tag. You never know how powerful your words can be to create peace.

With Love,
Alex

Made in the USA
Lexington, KY
15 August 2015